The hen said to the rat,
"I am big. You are little."

The cat said to the hen,
"I am big. You are little."

Big and Little

The rat said to the mouse,
"I am big. You are little."

The goat said,
"I am big. You are all little."

Along came a tiger.
"Who is big?" roared the tiger.

"You are big!" said the goat.
"You are big!" said the cat.
"You are big!" said the hen.
"You are big!" said the rat.

"I am little," said the mouse,
and it went into its hole.